D1164937

PRIVACY IN
THE DIGITAL AGE

IDENTITY
THEFT

BY A.W. BUCKEY

CONTENT CONSULTANT
Drew Procaccino, PhD
Associate Professor of Information Systems
Rider University

Core Library

Cover image: Protecting your devices with passwords
can help guard against identity theft.

An Imprint of Abdo Publishing
abdobooks.com

abdocorelibrary.com

Published by Abdo Publishing, a division of ABDO, PO Box 398166, Minneapolis, Minnesota 55439. Copyright © 2020 by Abdo Consulting Group, Inc. International copyrights reserved in all countries. No part of this book may be reproduced in any form without written permission from the publisher. Core Library™ is a trademark and logo of Abdo Publishing.

Printed in the United States of America, North Mankato, Minnesota
012019
092019

THIS BOOK CONTAINS
RECYCLED MATERIALS

Cover Photo: Tero Vesalainen/Shutterstock Images
Interior Photos: Tero Vesalainen/Shutterstock Images, 1; Shutterstock Images, 4–5, 13, 18, 24–25, 45; Colleen Long/AP Images, 6-7; iStockphoto, 8, 30–31, 36–37, 43; Monkey Business Images/Shutterstock Images, 10–11, 16–17; Red Line Editorial, 21, 32; Jacob Lund/Shutterstock Images, 22; Jeramey Lende/Shutterstock Images, 28

Editor: Maddie Spalding
Series Designer: Megan Ellis

Library of Congress Control Number: 2018965965

Publisher's Cataloging-in-Publication Data

Names: Buckey, A. W., author.
Title: Identity theft / by A. W. Buckey
Description: Minneapolis, Minnesota : Abdo Publishing, 2020 | Series: Privacy in the digital age | Includes online resources and index.
Identifiers: ISBN 9781532118920 (lib. bdg.) | ISBN 9781532173103 (ebook) | ISBN 9781644940839 (pbk.)
Subjects: LCSH: Identity theft--United States--Prevention--Juvenile literature. | Online identity theft--Juvenile literature. | Identity theft--Law and legislation--Juvenile literature. | Privacy, Right of-- United States--Juvenile literature. | Personal information management-- Juvenile literature.
Classification: DDC 005.8--dc23

CONTENTS

CHAPTER
ONE

OPERATION SWIPER

On October 7, 2011, New York law enforcement exposed a network of 111 thieves. These thieves had stolen the credit information of thousands of people. The police investigation into this theft was called Operation Swiper. The name came from the swipe of a credit card. The district attorney said that it was the largest credit card theft the department had ever seen. The thieves had stolen more than $13 million.

The thieves had a complex way of stealing goods. The key to their plan was identity theft. They had

Many people use credit cards to buy things. Credit information is part of a person's identity.

paid shop and restaurant employees to help them. The employees swiped customers' credit cards through a device called a skimmer. The skimmer stole credit card information. The thieves stored this stolen data. They bought fake credit cards. They used the stolen credit card numbers on the fake cards. The thieves used the cards to buy products, such as computers. They sold the products to make money.

The thieves called stores. They pretended to be the owners of the cards. They also made fake drivers licenses

SYNTHETIC IDENTITY THEFT

One common type of identity theft is synthetic identity theft. To synthesize something is to create it from different parts. Thieves steal pieces of people's identities and combine them with made-up facts. Thieves might steal one person's credit card information and another person's name. Then they combine the name and card information. In this way, thieves create new identities.

Skimmers are small devices that scan credit card information.

Passports and other documents contain important information about a person's identity.

and other forms of identification. This helped make the fake cards seem real.

IDENTITY THEFT

Identity is a word for the features that make us who we are. These features include a person's name, age, and background. Identity theft is the act of stealing another person's identity. Identity fraud is the use of this stolen information. Identity thieves usually use another person's identity to steal money, goods, or services.

Millions of Americans are affected by identity theft each year. Identity theft affects many parts of a victim's life. It can restrict the person's ability to do things, such as buy houses and get credit cards. But knowing the signs of identity theft can help prevent it from happening.

WHAT IS IDENTITY?

Who are you? There are many ways to answer this question. One way is with a name. Another is with a nationality or an occupation. Some people might answer with an internet username. All of these things are identities. A person's identity is made up of different features, or markers.

Some identity markers are shared by groups of people. For example, "Buddhist" is a religious identity claimed by millions of people. Other identity markers are unique to each person. For example, each human being has a different fingerprint. No two passports have the same number.

An occupation is one part of a person's identity.

11

IDENTITY MARKERS

In the 1930s, the US government invented Social Security numbers. Each US citizen has a different number. People use Social Security numbers to file tax returns each year. People who pay more taxes than they owe will get money back from their tax returns. A thief could use a stolen Social Security number to receive someone else's tax refund. A Social Security number is also needed to apply for a loan. Someone who steals a person's Social Security number can get a loan while

SHOULDER SURFING

Automated teller machines (ATMs) were invented in 1967. ATMs allow people to withdraw cash from a bank account without visiting a bank. An ATM user inserts a bank card. The user types in a secret code. The code gives the user access to a bank account. The ATM led to a type of identity theft called shoulder surfing. Shoulder surfers sneak up behind ATM users. They watch people type their ATM codes. They use this information to steal from a person's bank account.

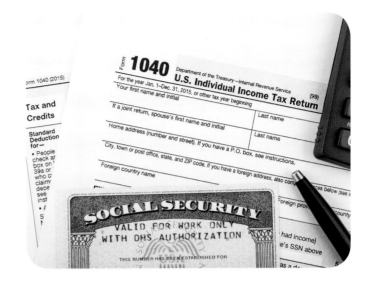

People use their social security numbers to fill out tax return forms.

pretending to be the other person. Then they never repay the loan.

Credit cards were invented in 1950. Consumers can buy things with credit cards. Each credit card has a different number. Today, credit card theft is the most reported type of identity theft.

THEFT IN THE DIGITAL AGE

In the 1990s, the internet became popular. Identity theft became common as more people used the internet. In 1998 the US government passed the Identity Theft and Assumption Deterrence Act. This law made identity theft a federal crime punishable by up to 15 years in prison.

The internet has made it easier for people to commit identity theft. Identity markers such as Social Security numbers are stored online. Companies track and sell information about their customers. In the past 15 years, identity theft has increased in the United States. Approximately 16.7 million Americans were victims of identity theft in 2017.

STRAIGHT TO THE
SOURCE

Lawyer Mari Frank is a victim of identity theft. She wrote a book about how victims can rebuild their lives after identity theft. In an interview, she explained how the internet has made identity theft easier:

> *In the olden days, you really [had] to actually go to maybe get court records or do some other things to commit identity theft. That would take much longer. So, yes, there was identity theft. And there were people who were able to do that as a profession, people who were very smart about getting your information—people like private investigators. . . . Now they put that [information] online. There are hundreds and hundreds of sites that you can go to. You don't have to spend a great deal of money or a great deal of time. It's transferred to you in just a second.*
>
> Source: "Interview: Mari Frank." *Frontline*. PBS, n.d. Web.
> Accessed October 24, 2018.

Back It Up

The author of this passage is using evidence to support a point. Write a paragraph describing the point the author is making. Then write down two or three pieces of evidence the author uses to make the point.

DIGITAL IDENTITY THEFT

dentity thieves often use three strategies to steal identity information. These strategies are phishing, malware, and hacking. Some identity thieves also create fake social media profiles. They steal photos online to make their profiles seem real. This tactic is called catfishing.

Many people have online accounts that contain personal information.

Many people use PayPal to pay for goods and services.

PHISHING

Phishing scams are carried out over the internet. These scams involve a tactic called social engineering. Thieves pretend to be an organization that the user trusts. They send emails pretending to be a business or the government. They ask people for identity information.

For example, identity thieves created a mass phishing scam in 2017. They sent an email to many people. The email appeared to be from the payment service PayPal. The PayPal logo was included in the email. The email told users that there was a problem with their PayPal account. It told them to log into their accounts immediately. People who clicked on the login link were taken to another site. The site looked just like PayPal's home page. The thieves hoped users would enter their account passwords into this new site. Then the thieves could get access to a user's PayPal account. PayPal accounts are usually linked to bank account and credit card data. In this way, thieves were able to steal many people's identities.

MALWARE

Malware is a type of software that infects a device or website. Malware collects information from the computers it infects. For example, a piece of malware might be attached to an online pop-up advertisement. Clicking on the ad installs and starts the malware program. The malware records everything that the person types. This can include a person's online passwords. Then the owner of the malware can use this information to steal the person's identity.

DATA BREACHES

Many organizations store data about their users. They collect and track identity markers such as Social Security numbers. Organizations use security systems to protect this data. But some people know how to beat these

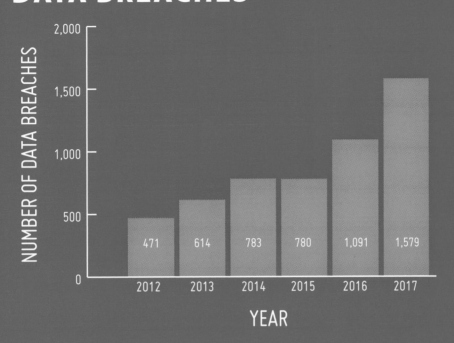

DATA BREACHES

NUMBER OF DATA BREACHES

Year	Number
2012	471
2013	614
2014	783
2015	780
2016	1,091
2017	1,579

YEAR

The above graph shows the number of data breaches in the United States in each year from 2012 to 2017. Experts predict that this number will continue to grow over time. Why do you think the number of breaches is growing each year? What could be done to stop this trend?

systems. They use phishing, malware, or other methods to steal the data. This process is called hacking.

The theft of secured data is called a data breach. Data breaches affect millions of people each year. A large data breach happened in 2017. Hackers breached the company Equifax. Equifax is a credit

The internet gives people access to information, but it has made identity theft easier.

reporting agency. It collects credit information to give people credit scores. A credit score gives information about how good a person is at managing debt and making payments on time.

The Equifax breach affected nearly half of all Americans. The hacked data included Social Security numbers. Thieves used this data to make fake credit accounts and get loans.

CATFISHING

Catfishing is a type of digital identity abuse. Catfish are people who steal personal information such as photos and names. They sometimes combine this information with made-up identity markers. Catfish use this information to create fake social media accounts.

Some catfish want friendship or romance with their victims. Other people catfish to commit crimes. For example, someone might steal the online photographs and life details of a sick person. The catfish pretends to be this person. Then the catfish might ask people to send money for medical bills. This is a type of identity fraud.

CATFISH

A documentary called *Catfish* was released in 2010. It is about a man named Nev Schulman. Schulman starts an online friendship with an eight-year-old painter named Abby. Schulman helps Abby sell her art. He begins an online romance with her half-sister Megan. Nev soon learns that neither person is real. "Abby" and "Megan" are both fake identities. A woman named Angela Wesselman created these identities. She had used photos of a family friend to create Megan's identity. Wesselman was unhappy in her real life. She wanted a relationship and more attention for her art. The movie introduced the term "catfishing."

CHAPTER
FOUR

THE HARM OF IDENTITY THEFT

The number of identity theft cases has increased over time. Experts think thefts will continue to increase. This is partly because so much information has already been stolen. Data breaches offer millions of theft opportunities. People might still be continuing to sell and buy data from large breaches.

Identity theft victims are usually not held responsible. They often do not have to pay back most of the purchases

Many identity theft victims suffer from stress and anxiety.

THE CON QUEEN OF HOLLYWOOD

One well-known identity thief is called the "Con Queen of Hollywood." Most people think this thief is a woman. The thief has spoken over the phone to victims. The thief's voice sounds like a woman's voice. She steals the identities of Hollywood producers. She makes a fake email address and website under a producer's name. She asks photographers and actors to lend her money for projects. But she never pays them back. Nicoletta Kotsianas has been investigating these scams. She says, "This woman learns everything there is to know about her targets. She tweaks her voice and accent and sounds like who she is impersonating."

made in their names. But identity theft can be damaging in other ways. In a 2017 survey of 176 identity theft victims, most victims reported feeling angry and betrayed. They were anxious about the future. Many of the victims had trouble sleeping. Most felt stressed. Identity theft can also damage a person's credit.

CREDIT DAMAGE

Credit is money loaned to a person or group. People pay back the money over time with interest. Credit is often used for large purchases. For example, most people cannot pay the price of a house all at once. They get a loan from a bank. This loan is called a mortgage. They make payments on their mortgage each month. These loans become part of a person's credit history.

CREDIT REPORT SCAMS

Some phishing scammers pose as credit reporting agencies. They send emails offering credit score information if a user enters personal data. This credit score offer is misleading. Scammers use the data to steal a person's identity. Only one reliable website offers a free annual credit score. This site is called AnnualCreditReport.com. The credit reporting agencies Experian, Equifax, and Transunion operate this site.

People usually get big loans from banks. Banks want to make sure their loans are repaid. They want to give loans to people who are likely to pay them back. They look at a person's credit history to find this information. People who pay back their loans on time have good credit.

People can view and track their credit scores online.

Credit reporting agencies track a person's credit. The three biggest US credit reporting agencies are Experian, Equifax, and Transunion. They give people credit scores. A high score means that a person has good credit. Identity theft can make a person's credit score go down. Identity thieves usually do not pay back the loans they take out. This hurts the victim's credit. Credit scores can be improved. But this process takes time. Victims need to make payments on time. Then they can slowly start to rebuild their credit history.

STRAIGHT TO THE
SOURCE

Terry Spencer had her identity stolen. In an interview, she described the damage the theft caused:

> I felt that it was a huge invasion of my privacy, my character, my life. It really surprised me just simply because I think that I'm one of those people that have gone through life with nothing bad happening to them, and this really shocked me. It just shocked me that someone had the nerve . . . to steal my identity and to become me. . . . Since I did have my identity stolen, I am a lot more diligent, and I do check my credit report and my credit ratings score on a much more frequent basis than I had in the past.

> Source: Kim McGrigg. "Interview with an ID Theft Victim."
> *Money Management International*. Money Management
> International, October 22, 2010. Web.
> Accessed October 24, 2018.

Consider Your Audience
Adapt this passage for a different audience, such as your friends. Write a blog post conveying this same information for the new audience. How does your post differ from the original text and why?

PREVENTION AND RESPONSE

dentity theft can happen to anyone. Strong passwords can help keep data safe. Passwords should be long. They should contain numbers and special characters like accent marks and currency symbols. Experts recommend that people create passphrases. A passphrase is a sentence that includes special characters and numbers. The first letters, numbers, and characters can be used to form a password. For example, a passphrase could be, "I went to Mexico on 7/1/2019!" Then the password would be "IwtMo712019!" People should never write down their passwords.

Passwords and personal identification numbers can help protect a person's banking accounts.

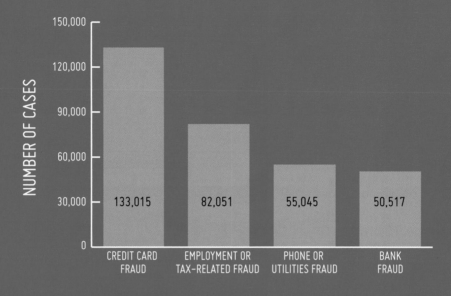

IDENTITY FRAUD IN 2017

NUMBER OF CASES

- 150,000
- 120,000
- 90,000
- 60,000
- 30,000
- 0

CREDIT CARD FRAUD	EMPLOYMENT OR TAX-RELATED FRAUD	PHONE OR UTILITIES FRAUD	BANK FRAUD
133,015	82,051	55,045	50,517

TYPES OF FRAUD

The above graph shows the most common types of identity fraud in 2017. Which type was most common? What do you think was the reason for this?

They should have a different password for each online account.

CHECKING CREDIT

United States law gives each citizen a free credit report once a year. This report shows whether the person has paid back loans. It keeps track of new accounts and debts. Credit report checks can help catch identity theft.

People can choose to pay for credit monitoring services. Credit card companies offer these services. They report suspicious credit card activity to the card's owner. Suspicious activity includes unusual purchases.

RESPONDING TO THEFT

When identity theft occurs, it is important

MULTI-FACTOR AUTHENTICATION

Multi-factor authentication (MFA) is a data security process. It requires people to verify their identities in different ways. Single-factor authentication might involve just typing a password. With MFA, a person may need to type in both a password and a security code that is texted to their phone. MFA is a feature that users can set up for extra security. It can help protect important information.

to respond quickly. Victims can report the theft to the government. They should contact one of the three major credit reporting agencies and freeze their credit. A credit freeze keeps thieves from using a person's credit. A credit reporting agency can temporarily unfreeze an account if the credit owner needs a loan.

People who think their credit card information has been stolen should let their credit card company know immediately. The company can freeze the card. This blocks new credit card purchases.

CHILD IDENTITY THEFT

Under federal law, children cannot take out loans or get credit cards. For this reason, children do not usually have credit scores and reports. Some identity thieves steal children's Social Security numbers. A thief can use this information to create new credit accounts. They can apply for credit cards or take out loans in the child's name.

Parents can check with credit reporting agencies to see if credit reports have been created in their children's names. Many states also allow parents to request credit reports for their children. The parent asks a credit reporting agency to create a report. Then the agency can freeze a child's credit. This prevents thieves from opening credit accounts in the child's name.

FURTHER EVIDENCE

Chapter Five talks about ways people can prevent and respond to identity theft. What was one of the main points of this chapter? What evidence is included to support this point? Read the article at the website below. Does the information on the website support this point? Or does it present new evidence?

ONLINE SAFETY
abdocorelibrary.com/identity-theft

Social Media

Facebook

Gmai

G+
Google+

You

IDENTITY THEFT PROTECTION

P eople around the world rely on the internet. But the internet is a risky place to keep identity data. Many people think the public should be given more information about data breaches.

POLICY CHANGES

Few laws address the problem of data breaches. Each US state has a data breach law. These laws require companies to tell people when their data is breached. But some of

Social media apps usually have privacy settings to help protect users' personal information.

these laws are not very effective. They do not cover all kinds of data. A company may not want to let customers know that its data was stolen. A data breach could indicate that a company has bad security. It could cause a company to lose customers. Weak data breach laws allow some companies to keep breaches secret. Some people argue for more data breach laws. They think people have a right to know about hacks.

BIOMETRIC DATA

People can use many layers of security to protect themselves. One type of security is something that a person knows, such as a password. Another type of security is something that a person has, such as a passport. But passwords can be forgotten. Something that a person owns can be lost. Biometric scans can provide another layer of security. In a biometric scan, a device scans part of a person's body. Each person's body has unique identity markers, such as fingerprints. These are called biometric markers. A device can scan a person's finger to get fingerprint information. A person's fingerprint could be used instead of a password. Some devices use facial recognition technology. Each person has different facial features. The device scans a person's face to confirm the person's identity. This technology has been developed for smartphones. The smartphone remains locked until the user's face is recognized.

Some people think biometric data could reduce identity theft. Stealing this data is much harder

EYE SCANS

One biometric marker comes from a person's eyes. Each person has a unique blood vessel pattern inside the eye. Technology can match this pattern to a person. This process is called an eye scan. One type of eye scan is an iris scan. The iris is the colored part of a person's eye. Another type of eye scan is a retinal scan. The retina is the part of the eye that converts light into images. These special scans look at different parts of the eye. Some banks use retinal scans. Customers scan their eyes instead of providing a password.

than hacking. Others believe that biometric data is risky. People can change a hacked password. But they cannot change their biometric data. A data breach of a biometric system could be very dangerous. The information the thieves steal could not be replaced.

Identity theft is a common crime. The internet has made identity theft easier to commit. No one's identity is completely safe from theft. But protective measures can reduce the risk of identity theft.

The future of identity theft is unknown. Identity theft may become more commonplace. But new protective technologies may help reduce the rate of identity theft. Protecting a person's identity is a major challenge. Lawmakers and technology developers are just beginning to tackle it.

EXPLORE ONLINE

Chapter Six discusses some ways to protect people from identity theft. The article at the website below gives more information on this topic. How is the information from the website similar to information in this chapter? What new information did you learn from the website?

IDENTITY THEFT
abdocorelibrary.com/identity-theft

FAST FACTS

- A person's identity is made up of many markers. Some parts of a person's identity, such as a nationality, are shared. Others, such as a passport number, are unique to each person.

- Identity theft is the act of stealing some or all of a person's identity. Thieves often steal identities in order to commit a crime.

- Identity theft is becoming more common over time. Approximately 16.7 million Americans were victims of identity theft in 2017. The internet has made identity theft easier to commit.

- Common digital identity theft strategies include phishing, malware, hacking, and catfishing.

- Password protection and credit monitoring can help prevent identity theft.

- Victims of identity theft should immediately contact federal agencies, credit reporting agencies, and credit card companies.

- Some lawmakers are looking into new policies for protecting consumer privacy. Others are looking to biometric data as a new form of identity protection.

STOP AND
THINK

Tell the Tale

Chapter Four of this book discusses the effects of identity theft. Imagine that you have been a victim of identity theft. Write 200 words about the experience. In what ways would you try to protect yourself and your identity?

Surprise Me

Chapter Three talks about some of the most common ways people commit digital identity theft. After reading this book, what two or three facts about digital identity theft did you find most surprising? Write a few sentences about each fact. Why did you find each fact surprising?

Say What?

Studying identity theft can mean learning a lot of new vocabulary. Find five words in this book you've never heard before. Use a dictionary to find out what they mean. Then write the meanings in your own words and use each word in a new sentence.

Another View

Chapter Two talks about the history of identity theft. As you know, every source is different. Ask an adult to help you find another source about this topic. Write a short essay comparing and contrasting the new source's point of view with that of this book's author. What is the point of view of each author? How are they similar and why? How are they different and why?

GLOSSARY

biometric data
information that comes
from the human body, such
as fingerprints

credit
loans from a bank or credit
card company

credit report
a record of a person's
credit history

debt
money that a person owes

hacking
the act of breaking through
data security systems in
order to find protected data

identity
the markers that make up
who a person is

interest
a fee for borrowing money

loan
money that is borrowed

ONLINE
RESOURCES

To learn more about identity theft, visit our free resource websites below.

Visit **abdocorelibrary.com** or scan this QR code for free Common Core resources for teachers and students, including vetted activities, multimedia, and booklinks, for deeper subject comprehension.

Visit **abdobooklinks.com** or scan this QR code for free additional online weblinks for further learning. These links are routinely monitored and updated to provide the most current information available.

LEARN
MORE

Gifford, Clive. *Computer Networks*. New York: Crabtree Publishing, 2015.

Smibert, Angie. *Inside Computers*. Minneapolis, MN: Abdo Publishing, 2019.

INDEX

About the Author

A.W. Buckey is a writer living in Brooklyn, New York.